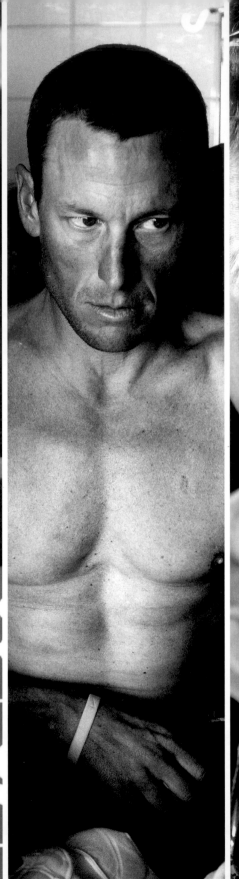

UP

CLOSE

AND

PERSONAL

COMEBACK 2.0

LANCE ARMSTRONG

PHOTOGRAPHS BY ELIZABETH KREUTZ

A TOUCHSTONE BOOK
Published by Simon & Schuster

New York   London   Toronto   Sydney

For Luke, Grace, Bella, and Max—for continuing to be
the ones to inspire me every second of every day.

Love, Dad

For my husband, James. You have always encouraged me to follow
my passion and your partnership has helped make this project
possible. I love you.

—E.K.

Touchstone
A Division of Simon & Schuster, Inc.
1230 Avenue of the Americas
New York, NY 10020

This Touchstone hardcover edition November 2009

TOUCHSTONE and colophon are registered trademarks of Simon & Schuster, Inc.

For information about special discounts for bulk purchases, please contact Simon & Schuster Special Sales at 1-866-506-1949 or business@simonandschuster.com.

The Simon & Schuster Speakers Bureau can bring authors to your live event. For more information or to book an event contact the Simon & Schuster Speakers Bureau
at 1-866-248-3049 or visit our website at www.simonspeakers.com.

Designed by Ruth Lee-Mui

Manufactured in the United States of America

1   3   5   7   9   10   8   6   4   2

ISBN 978-1-4391-8435-6

The view from the top of the final podium

in the Tour de France is pretty sweet. It was particularly sweet in July 2005, when I was celebrating my seventh consecutive Tour win. I'd accomplished what I'd set out to do. An eighth attempt held no allure for me. As much as I love competition— and winning—and even the demands of training, I was ready for a break.

In 1997, after I recovered from the testicular cancer that had metastasized to my abdomen, lungs, and brain, I felt as though I deserved a permanent vacation. I did take one for a while. I played a lot of golf and drank a fair amount of beer. But that lifestyle played itself out for me after about six months and I found my way back to competitive cycling.

After that 2005 Tour I wasn't really feeling the urge for a permanent vacation, but I was eager to get back to the things that training had kept me away from—chiefly my three kids. Luke, Bella, and Grace had had to deal with my being away during the long months of training required for successful Tour campaigns. I was eager to spend more time with them. I was also eager to work more actively for the Lance Armstrong Foundation, the organization that I'd started to help other cancer survivors and people battling the disease. (I would also work hard on getting Proposition 15 passed in Texas—the first state initiative to finance cancer research.) I also needed a break. Call it a mini-permanent vacation.

In 2006 and 2007, the Tour de France wasn't really on my radar. I wasn't avoiding it; it just wasn't on the front burner for me. Between my kids, lobbying for cancer research, and training for several marathons, my life was plenty full. But in July 2008, I was staying at the Blackwell Hotel in Columbus, Ohio, for the 2008 LIVE**STRONG** Summit, and my friend and manager Mark Higgins and I found ourselves with a lot of downtime in the mornings before conference events got going. Somewhat surprisingly, our hotel TV got Versus, the channel that covers the Tour pretty much 24/7 every July. Given this chance, I quickly dialed in. What got to me was watching the stage when they climbed Alpe d'Huez. I have history with Alpe d'Huez. Good history. Most notably when I won a Stage 16 time trial there that was critical to my 2004 Tour victory.

As I watched Carlos Sastre make his move on Alpe d'Huez, a move that went essentially unchallenged, I felt a pang: I want back in. It was the first time I'd even considered a return to the Tour de France. I can't say that I decided right then and there to mount a comeback, but the seed was planted. In the days and weeks that followed, it was on my mind. Increasingly on my mind.

About this same time I was training for the Leadville Trail 100, a tough 100-mile mountain bike race in Leadville, Colorado. I'd originally planned to do this race in 2007. My friend and coach Chris Carmichael was going to do it, and then a bunch of us decided that we'd all do it and the guy with the slowest time

would buy dinner for the rest. But after Floyd Landis announced that he was going to do Leadville, the media started pitting us against each other. I didn't like the feel of that, so I decided against doing the race that time. But I stayed interested and trained for it the following year.

Chris was coaching me. One day we were riding together and I said, "What if we keep it going after Leadville?"

"I think there's another long mountain bike race in British Columbia in September," Chris said.

"No," I said. "What if we did the Tour?"

Chris shot me a look. "You're kidding."

"Maybe. Maybe not."

Chris was genuinely stunned. He also didn't think it was a good idea. For one thing, he said, most comebacks don't work. If I didn't win, I'd go out losing. I guess he was worried about my "legacy." Later, my business partner Bart Knaggs expressed the same concern. Chris asked me to give it more thought.

Don't get me wrong. I'm very proud of winning seven consecutive Tours de France. But there's no way I'm going to let that "legacy" stop me from putting myself on the line again. For one thing, my legacy—whatever it is—can't be worth much if a lesser result would somehow tarnish it. Second, I can't let myself become paralyzed for fear of jeopardizing what I've achieved so far. For me, living life to the fullest is a lot about testing myself: accepting challenges, training hard, and then going for it. No way I'm spending the rest

of my days avoiding goals. As far as I'm concerned, that would wreck my legacy.

When I mentioned the possibility of a comeback to Mark Higgins, he took it calmly—not a surprise if you know the guy. He reminded me that when I retired I was all about my kids. Luke, Bella, and Grace were next on my list to tell—but only after I'd told their mother, Kristin.

Kristin and I had a family vacation with the kids in Santa Barbara. On the way home to Austin, I told her there was something I wanted to run by her. When I explained my desire for a comeback, she cried—I think in part because I asked her and partly in relief; she'd thought I was going to say I wanted to run for office. She was fine about my coming out of retirement. I'd have her support.

My kids knew about my history with the Tour, but at this point it was more through what friends had told them than from anything they actually remembered. So they were excited about the prospect of living through it with me and going to France.

Two days after he'd asked me to think about it, I called Chris Carmichael back to let him know I was doing it. I asked him if he wanted to work with me. "Dude," he said, "what do you think?" Chris had just wanted me to consider the pros and cons, but once I'd made my decision, he was with me all the way. It was a relief. It's hard to imagine training without Chris's expertise.

I also couldn't imagine launching a comeback

of any kind without Johan Bruyneel. Johan was the directeur sportif—the guy in charge—of my team in all of the Tours that I won. He himself is a former pro cyclist and Tour de France veteran who once outsprinted the great champion Miguel Indurain in a stage that ended in Johan's native Belgium. In the years since, he's become a brilliant team strategist—truly unparalleled in our sport. Small wonder he's been the architect of so many team and individual victories in the Tour de France.

Like everyone else I confided in at this time, Johan didn't know whether or not to take me seriously. He wound up flying to Austin pretty much to look me in the eye to see if I was for real. He instantly saw that I was.

Johan was set to direct the Astana squad, a cycling team based in Kazakhstan, in the 2009 Tour, and he already had an amazing lineup. I was pretty frank with him. I didn't want to keep him from working with a guy who might dominate the Tour for the next several years to work with me for maybe just one. But Johan said that to him, working with me again would be more satisfying than working for the next five years with a potentially dominant Tour force. So we were good. And I couldn't have been more heartened by Johan's great friendship and confidence in me.

Right around this time I called Bill Stapleton, a former Olympic swimmer who's been my longtime agent. Bill has had my back for so long, I don't remember when he didn't have it. When I had cancer, he was

the guy who kept the director of Cofidis, my Tour team then, at bay when the guy arrived with the false gift of a bottle of wine, determined to renegotiate the terms of my contract or force me to take a physical when I was lying in a hospital bed, sick from chemo.

I'd started texting Bill about the Tour right after watching that Alpe d'Huez stage. At first he thought I was joking. "Put down your beer and go back to the beach" pretty much sums up his reaction. But when he realized that I was serious, he took me seriously. His only real question was, "Do you really want to suffer like that again?" It was a good question. Because suffering is what bike racing is really all about. And the one who can suffer the most usually wins. Once I said yeah, I was ready, Bill's reaction was simple—and close to the Nike motto: "Let's do it," he said. And he began to put in motion all the steps necessary for my return, from clearing my schedule to finding me a team.

The cancer survivor movement is never far from my mind. I happened to receive the Lance Armstrong Foundation board packet for our upcoming Columbus summit right around the time that the 2008 Tour was starting. It had given me a lot to think about.

The LAF had just completed two years of research focused on views about cancer in twenty-five foreign countries. The results were staggering: Stigma about having cancer was still common in both developed and developing nations. Many people think that cancer is contagious. Even more important, at that time there was

no individual or organization leading the charge globally for those dealing with cancer. At our Columbus summit, we planned to discuss the launch of an awareness campaign with global reach.

I got on the phone with Doug Ulman, a three-time cancer survivor who is the president of the LAF, and asked if my comeback could help boost this global initiative. While he was at Brown University, Doug had survived chondrosarcoma and then two malignant melanomas. He came back to help Brown's soccer team win three Ivy League championships. Since then he's completed ten marathons—and one 100-mile race in the Himalayas. I've heard of altitude training, but altitude racing? Crazy.

Doug was immediately enthusiastic. He said that my comeback could help a lot. So right from the start, as my training and racing plans began to take shape, Doug helped me form an itinerary that would have me meeting with cancer patients around the globe as well as with the foreign leaders who have a lot to say about making cancer research a priority. My goal would be threefold: to raise awareness about cancer, the number-one cause of death worldwide; to reduce the stigma still attached to the disease and to let people know that it is survivable; and to ignite a grass-roots movement around the world. I'm proud to say that the LAF's global initiative now extends to sixty-five countries.

Only later did I think about doing this book. I realized what a great opportunity this would be to share my comeback story with others in a visual way—to really give people a look at my life from the inside. And I mean all of my life: training, racing, goofing off, raising my kids, working for people battling cancer.

I probably wouldn't have thought of doing a book like this if it weren't for Elizabeth Kreutz. I met Liz more than fifteen years ago when I first moved to Austin. She was the second employee of the Lance Armstrong Foundation. She's like a sister to me, and she's become an incredibly accomplished photographer. She has covered two Olympic Games and five Tours de France and her work has appeared in many publications including Sports Illustrated and Newsweek. There is no other photographer of her caliber whom I would have been comfortable letting into my life. I can be completely myself around Liz. So in the pages that follow, that's what you'll get: a true-to-life, behind-the-scenes look at this 2009 comeback of mine.

Can I come back and win again? I'm going to give it a shot, but in some respects the winning-or-losing aspect of it doesn't matter as much now. What matters most is continuing to dream the dream: to envision challenges, take them on, try your best, and let the chips fall. You don't have to have been near death to know that that's what living is all about—but maybe it helps.

Enjoy!

—Lance Armstrong
May 2009

Decision Made, Telling the World, Preparing for the Comeback

SEPTEMBER 2008

I started to put in longer training rides this month. Heading out of my ranch in Drippings Springs, Texas, on an old farm road going toward Johnson City, I saw what looked like a dog in the distance. As I got closer I realized it wasn't a dog, it was a pig—just standing out in the middle of the road all by himself. The truck behind me is Dave Bloch's truck; he was following me on my training ride that day. Johnson City happens to be the birthplace and hometown of President Lyndon B. Johnson. When Johnson was president a lot of the old dirt roads around there inexplicably got paved—so they're great for riding. You can see here I wasn't yet serious about cycling: I still have hairy legs.

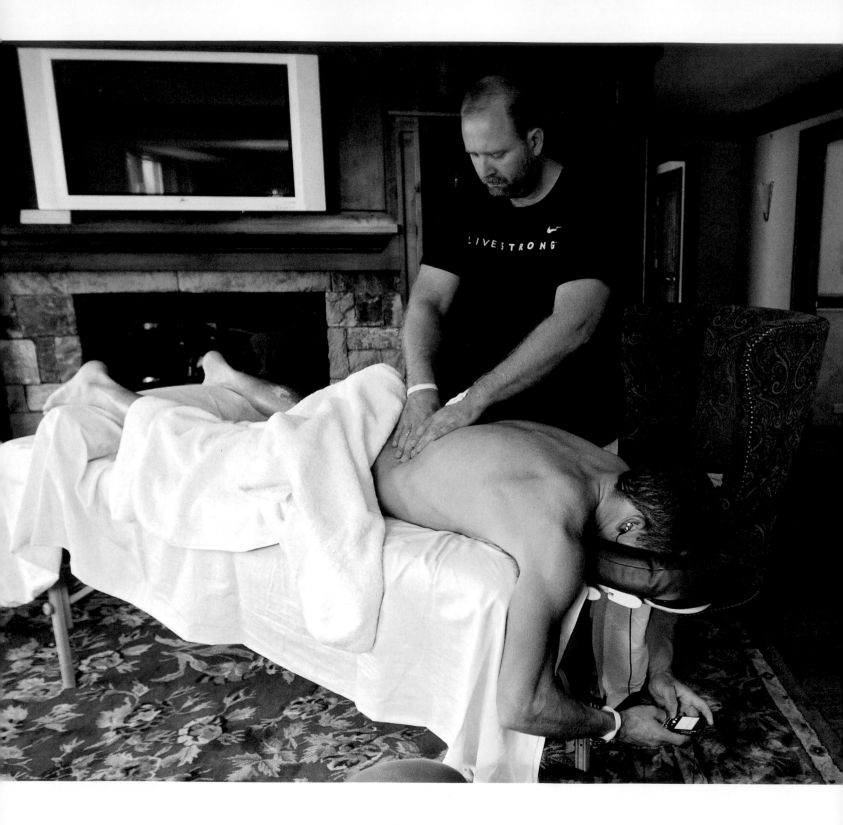

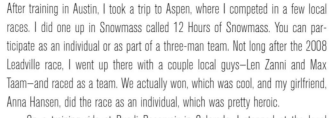

After training in Austin, I took a trip to Aspen, where I competed in a few local races. I did one up in Snowmass called 12 Hours of Snowmass. You can participate as an individual or as part of a three-man team. Not long after the 2008 Leadville race, I went up there with a couple local guys—Len Zanni and Max Taam—and raced as a team. We actually won, which was cool, and my girlfriend, Anna Hansen, did the race as an individual, which was pretty heroic.

On a training ride at Ruedi Reservoir in Colorado, I stopped at the local store to get a cold drink and the Associated Press called to confirm that I was making a comeback.

While in New York for the Clinton Global Initiative, I visited a handful of TV shows to announce my comeback and my yearlong commitment to the Global Cancer Campaign. I love being a guest on <u>Late Show with David Letterman</u>. Dave is always funny and the studio audience is great.

I was waiting to go on a morning show, and this fan wanted to take my picture, but obviously my mind was on something else.

With Diane Sawyer and Julianne Moore. Diane is one of my favorite people in the American media-scape—very smart and always pleasant to be around. That same day I visited the set of CNN's <u>American Morning</u>.

After the television shows, it was time to get ready to speak at the Clinton Global Initiative. Doug Ulman, the president of the Lance Armstrong Foundation, and I always compete for who can tie the best knot.

At the kickoff of CGI it was quite an honor for me to be standing there with arguably two of the most powerful men in the world, Mayor Bloomberg and President Clinton.

I got to spend some time with President Clinton and President Bush Senior. Despite their history as political adversaries, the two have become great friends and have partnered for things like tsunami relief efforts and Katrina survivor support. It's so heartening to see a rivalry deeply transformed in the service of such good causes.

After traveling to New York for my comeback announcement, we flew to Las Vegas for CrossVegas—a cyclo-cross race. While there I attended the Interbike trade show. A huge crowd showed up there for a signing at the Oakley booth.

After Vegas, we landed in Austin. I picked up a lot of gear in Vegas. What the heck I am supposed to do with this pile of wheels?

OCTOBER 2008

A typical off-season workout for me: a lot of core, full-body, and stability work. Last winter I was doing a lot of clapping push-ups, plyometrics, and some muscle-specific work with weights. I have a makeshift gym set up in my garage in Austin so I can do it all right there.

I had the opportunity to speak to the University of Texas football team before the Oklahoma State game last year. Coach Mack Brown and Colt McCoy were there when I addressed the entire team. On the way out, Luke and his buddy Jack Norman saw the door to the field, so they made for it and ran. Kids love to rip on grass and really feel free. I'm not any different, so we all ran as fast as we could, as if we were catching a touchdown pass from Colt McCoy.

We like to use our backyard to play football, soccer, tag, monkey in the middle—
a great way to spend time outdoors with your kids.

The LIVE**STRONG** Challenge Austin—formerly the Ride for the Roses—has been an Austin tradition for more than a decade. It started long ago around Valentine's Day as an informal race. The winner got two dozen roses to take home for his lady for Valentine's Day. It has morphed into a benefit for the Lance Armstrong Foundation, and last year Willie Nelson was gracious enough to come and play a set. Willie is truly a Texas legend, but it took absolutely no persuasion to get him to come out and perform at this event.

During the LIVE**STRONG** Challenge weekend I get to ride with some of our fund-raisers in a few smaller rides. With me here is Cindy Graf of Virginia Beach. Cindy's nonprofit, A Dolphin's Promise, in honor of her mom, Pat, who lost her battle with colon cancer, has raised $126,000 for LIVE**STRONG**.

NOVEMBER 2008

The Tour de Gruene is a classic Texas race. The course runs by Gruene Hall, a famous old live-music venue. Many of the country-western stars that we know today, from Pat Green to Willie Nelson, have played in Gruene Hall.

This race is special to me for two reasons. I did it as team LIVE**STRONG** this year with one of my best buds, John "College" Korioth, and won. And I did it in 1996, a month after I was diagnosed with cancer. I was weak, tired, and bald. Eddy Merckx, the greatest cyclist of all time, flew from Belgium to ride with me in that Tour de Gruene.

At this year's Tour de Gruene my daughter Grace had a good time playing photographer.

I try to be somewhat scientific in my approach to racing, so trials in the wind tunnel in San Diego are an important part of my prep routine. I test various positions to see which is the fastest for the time trial. Sometimes these wind tunnel tests don't translate exactly to the road, but they're close enough that the resulting information is valuable. Everything is taken into consideration: my position on the bike, the frame, the wheels, helmet, clothes, glasses, shoe covers, you name it.

DECEMBER 2008

Leading up to spring races, we always run a camp in December. This isn't a time to be too intensive in training; it's too early in the season. So we always do a variety of activities off the bike. We keep it fun but physical. In the past, the camp has been held in Austin, but in '08 we went to Tenerife, one of the Canary Islands. The day I was designated to pick the activity I found a local surf school and took the boys out on the water.

The media were all over our December training in Tenerife. Chechu Rubiera, my former teammate and longtime friend, couldn't be bothered by it all.

Between training and surfing, I found time to check out shoe designs for the **LIVESTRONG** collection that Fred Herlitz and Margie Wargo from Nike wanted to show me. Here I'm studying an old-school Nike cross-trainer that John McEnroe and Andre Agassi popularized years ago. Nike often reintroduces old favorites, giving them a modern twist and more modern colors.

Throughout the season I enjoyed the help of Gianluca Carretta, who kept me as straight as possible.

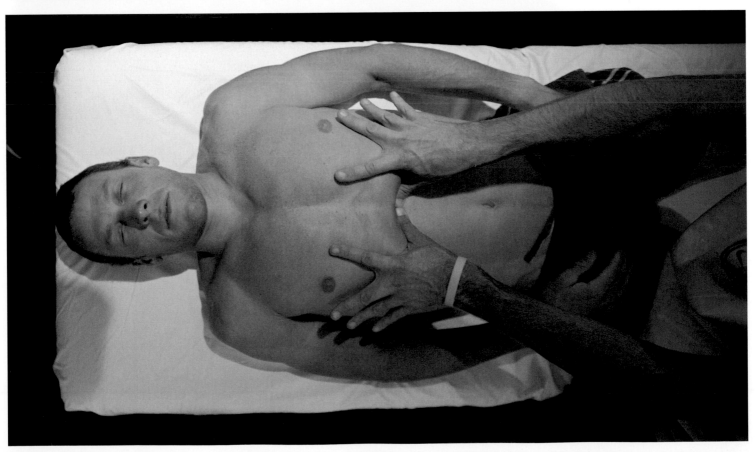

Even in December we look for challenging rides. We found what we were looking for on Tenerife, in the tiny town of Masca. This was a very, very demanding ride, probably the steepest road on the island, with about a 20 percent grade. Jani Brajkovic and I had to work to catch Levi Leipheimer and Jesús Hernández after they simulated a breakaway.

This was probably as friendly as it got between me and Alberto Contador, at a press conference on Tenerife. The media turnout was huge—hundreds of press representatives from all over the world.

Finally back in Austin. I never miss an opportunity to drop off my kids and pick them up at school when I'm in town. I think they look forward to the daily tradition; I know I do. Their school is about three minutes from our house. We get up, feed them breakfast, make their lunches, and throw them in the car. We're off to school by 7:45 a.m. Then I'm back in the carpool line at 2:45 p.m. to pick them up.

The kids' mom, Kristin; and Luke; Grace; Anna; and I cheered Bella on as she participated in a local children's cross-country race.

First Races,
Spreading the Cancer Message

JANUARY 2009

In January 2009, we went to the big island of Hawaii. They have the Ironman World Championship triathlon in Kona, which I hope to do someday. Every day in Hawaii I saw this cyclist in the pink top. I'd give her a little wave; she'd wave back.

Chris Carmichael, my longtime coach, took me out for intensive training sessions. He likes to stay close beside me to monitor everything I'm doing. This particular day we did a climb called Kaloko. It's very, very difficult, with pitches close to 25 percent. The climb extends for about 10 miles and ends up at 5,000 feet above sea level.

Still in Hawaii, I had just finished lunch with my kids when my phone rang. It was Jimmy Iovine from Interscope Records. He said Dr. Dre was in the office and wanted to catch up and wish me luck on my comeback. I went to find a seat out in the yard, but the only chairs around were these kiddie seats so I made myself at home.

I wasn't prepared to see myself on buses and billboards everywhere when I arrived in Adelaide, Australia, for the 2009 Tour Down Under. Every time I rode I would glance over, see my face, and nearly fall off my bike.

We went a week early and stayed in a family's private home, where I was able to iChat with my kids. A day or two later, after checking into the race hotel, the man who owned the house called me and said, "Hey, I'm in my kitchen and your kids just started iChatting. They just popped up on the screen and they're like, 'Who are you? Where's my daddy?' So I called to say your kids are looking for you." Halfway around the world. Pretty funny.

While in Adelaide I met with the premier of South Australia, Mike Rann, who has been supportive of LIVE**STRONG**. Here he is presenting me with a beautiful piece of Australian art.

My hair was getting a little long before the race, so I took the opportunity to cut it. I like to cut my own hair most of the time. I always need a little help in the back, so on this occasion I asked photographer Liz Kreutz for help. Clearly she shouldn't quit her day job. You can't see it here, but she wound up leaving me with a pretty nasty bald spot in the back.

The turnout at the team presentation for the Tour Down Under was huge. Paul Sherwen and Phil Liggett, the classic cycling color commentators, were on hand and interviewed me. This event was a prelude for the circuit race held two days before the start of the Tour Down Under, but already there were massive crowds.

This was the first team meeting for the comeback. It was great to be sitting in a room with all of the riders as well as Sean Yates, our director for the race. Sean is an old teammate and he was my mentor when I first turned pro in 1992. We were roommates from 1992 to 1996 when we were on the road for the races. It felt great to be working with him again.

After each stage I was interviewed by the media. They were curious about how the legs felt. On the right you see Diane Pucin of the <u>Los Angeles Times</u>.

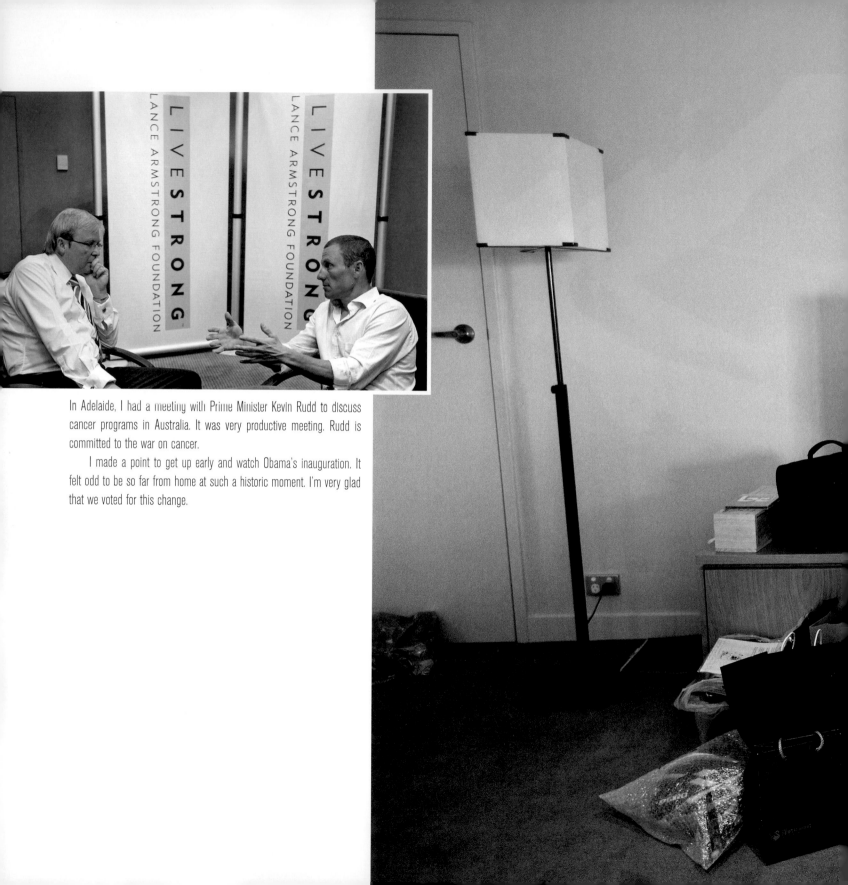

In Adelaide, I had a meeting with Prime Minister Kevin Rudd to discuss cancer programs in Australia. It was very productive meeting. Rudd is committed to the war on cancer.

I made a point to get up early and watch Obama's inauguration. It felt odd to be so far from home at such a historic moment. I'm very glad that we voted for this change.

In Texas you see signs that warn about cattle, sheep, and deer, but in Australia the alerts are for kangaroos. Riding on what feels like the wrong side of the road is pretty surreal, too. Australia was a great place to start my comeback, and I'm looking forward to next year's Tour Down Under.

FEBRUARY 2009

In February 2009 we went to training camp in Santa Rosa, California, in the Sonoma Valley, made famous by acres and acres of some of the best vineyards in the world. Levi's hometown is Santa Rosa, so he lobbied for us to go there. He promised us great roads, and he delivered. The weather was outstanding when we first arrived—though that was about to change, just in time for the AMGEN Tour of California.

The weather took a turn for the nasty, cold, and wet, but Jani Brajkovic and I still went out to train. Jani's been a great training partner this season. Really enjoyed the time I've been able to spend with him. This was a brutal climb.

During training camp we were paid a visit by the anti-doping inspectors. The level of oversight is intense. You are always accompanied to the bathroom by at least one inspector—you can't just walk into a bathroom alone with a cup and walk out with a sample. And your pants have to be down around your knees so they can see that no device was used to somehow switch samples.

It's humiliating and embarrassing, but it goes with the territory. The inspectors are in charge and like to have everything done their way. On this occasion the inspector wanted to give me tips for getting the bottle into the bag. I reminded him that nobody has put that bottle in a plastic bag and stuffed it into a Styrofoam container more often than I have.

In the past few years, blood testing has become an integral part of antidoping efforts. As methods of cheating have become more sophisticated, by necessity the screenings designed to detect them have had to become more comprehensive. At a press conference at the Tour of California, Irish reporter Paul Kimmage wanted to know why I am so "lenient" on former dopers. Kimmage takes issue with my belief that if a cyclist who was doping serves his sentence, he should be allowed to race again. I feel that once you've done your time, you can come back and stay as long as you're clean. I just don't believe in the "death" penalty when it comes to doping. Kimmage seems to have a problem with that.

We had unusually cold and very wet weather for the Tour of California in February. On an otherwise miserable day, nothing lifts my spirits like a Snickers bar. Not quite the lunch of champions, but it will do the trick.

A few of our bikes were stolen from the back of the team truck while we were in Sacramento, including the bike I use for time trials. The police came to take fingerprints and interview the mechanics and team directors. At that time I had 100,000 Twitter followers. I put up what amounted to an APB for the stolen goods. In the end, we got the bikes back and the suspects were apprehended—through the efforts of the Sacramento Police Department.

Even in bad weather, the natural beauty of northern California is impossible to suppress. But the roads remained wet, very slippery, and challenging. Each night we had to dry everything out in time for the next day's stage. Nobody wants to start the day with wet gear. It's always nice to have a fireplace to speed the process along.

The weather cleared before the fifth stage, across the Central Valley and past the almond groves. Levi and I rode side by side. I was pleased to see him win his third consecutive Tour of California. He was clearly the best on the hills and in the time trials—a very deserving winner.

Huge crowds turned out for the Tour of California. This particular climb—a tough one—is Palomar Mountain. It's long, steep, and goes up quite high. I have history here too: when I was a young triathlete training in San Diego, most of my rides took me out this way. I first climbed Palomar in 1986. It was cool to go back twenty years later and do it again.

After a hard stage they had some pizza waiting in the room. Like the Snickers bar, after a long day, warm pizza seemed like just what the doctor ordered.

On the podium with Levi, proud to be there with him in a supporting role.

Travels, Campaigns, and a Setback

03

MARCH 2009

In March, we made a trip to Mexico City to visit President Felipe Calderón and start the Tour of Mexico—Vuelta Mexico—which begins in Oaxaca. It turns out that President Calderón is an avid cyclist. When we met, he'd recently broken his collarbone, so we talked about that. Little did I know then that I would soon be in the very same position. We discussed the fight against cancer as well as other issues his country is facing right now. After our talk, we did an event for a group of kids at his residence, Los Piños.

Next we flew to Oaxaca to meet with the Trek-LIVE**STRONG** U23 team, which was getting ready for the tour, and I got a chance to catch up with the young guys. Axel Merckx, handing out race books, is an old teammate of mine and Eddy's son.

Before I left I took time to send a few postcards to my kids. They love receiving mail from other countries, so I always write to them when I'm abroad.

The pinewood derby is one of the most important races of the year. Luke and I were committed to building what we hoped would be the fastest car of all. We spent months planning the car and talking to people, pulling from their expertise. I'm proud to say that Luke did almost all of the designing, building, sanding, and refining himself. The car had to weigh exactly five ounces. On race day, Luke took first in one heat, but it's best of four. He wound up with one bad run: his car hit a bump and bounced off the track. You get a redo when that happens. On that try Luke's car hit the same bump and the car held to the track but it definitely slowed down. In spite of the bumps in the road, Luke took third, and we were both happy.

We headed out to Los Angeles to do an event downtown with Nike CEO Mark Parker. Shepard Fairey, left, is a contemporary artist perhaps best known for his arresting "hope" image of Barack Obama. Inspired by some of Liz's photos, he created similar portraits of me for this mural behind us.

While I was in L.A. I visited Childrens Hospital Los Angeles. It's tough seeing youngsters like Tsiana and Jonathon facing cancer. But visits like this and time spent with their parents only deepen my resolve to advance the LIVE**STRONG** message. Nothing inspires me more than these tough little kids.

Doug Ulman, Mark Parker, and I discussed the Lance Armstrong Foundation and Nike's commitment to the global fight against cancer. After that my good friend Ben Harper and his new band, Relentless7, played a set.

After L.A. we headed to Italy for the Milan–San Remo, a one-day race, and you can see it was a beautiful day.

I was happy to be racing in Europe again. From San Remo we went to Spain for the Vuelta a Castilla y León. This race sparked a lot of interest and anticipation because it was the first time I would share the road and the team with Alberto Contador.

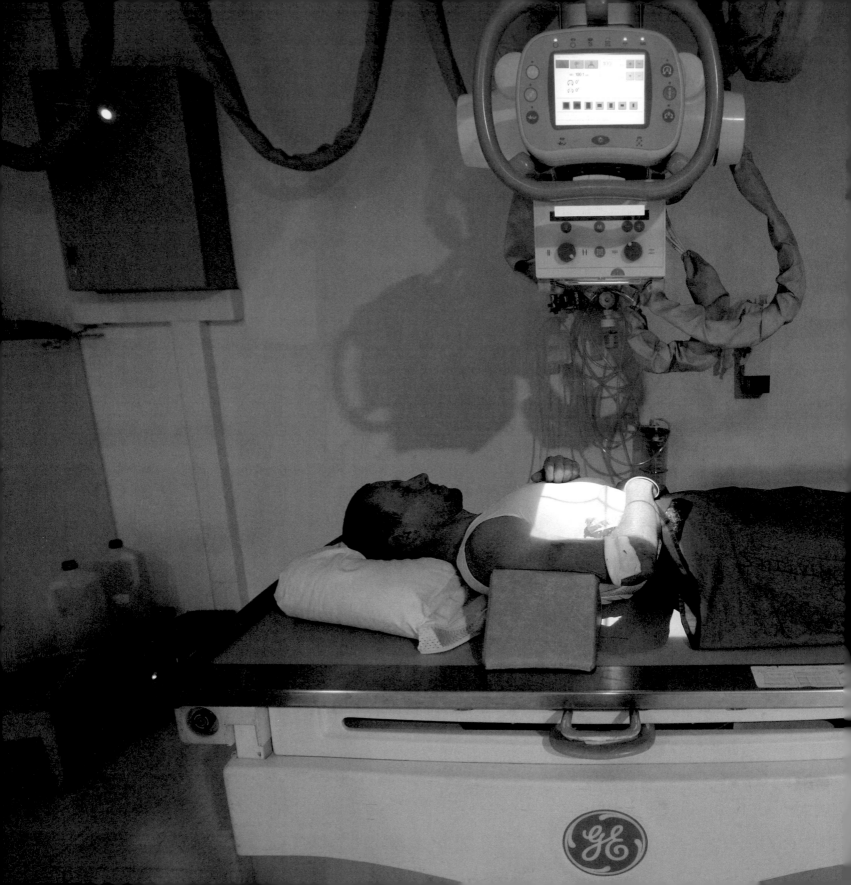

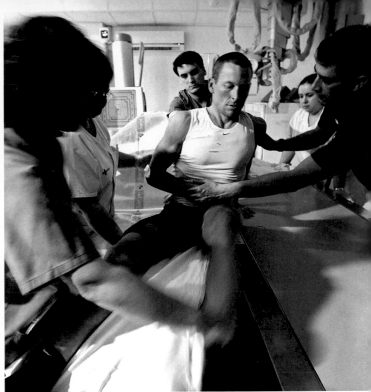

On day one of Vuelta a Castilla y León, I got caught in the back when some guys crashed in front of me. I couldn't avoid them, went over the bars, and landed pretty hard on my right shoulder. X-rays were taken at the hospital in Spain. Diagnosis: my collarbone was broken in a few places. I was in total misery, still wearing the socks and cycling shorts from the race. Moving around was not fun. Very painful.

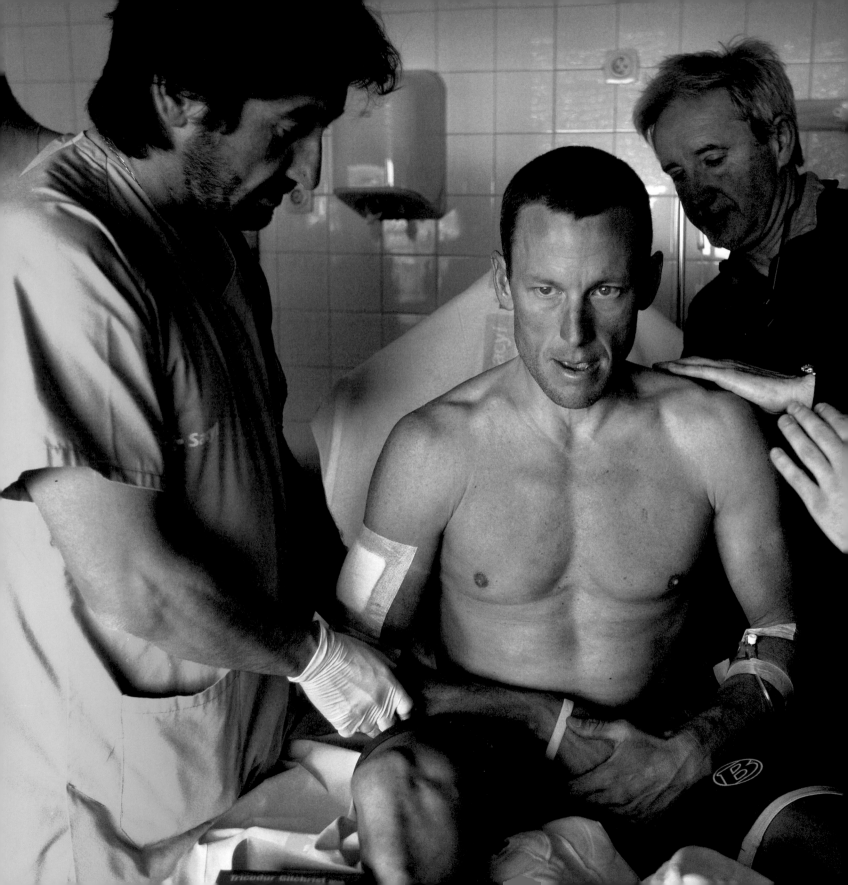

The doctors from the hospital continued to examine me. Our team doctor, Pedro Celaya, kept a close eye on the procedures. He is a wonderful man and a true friend. It was comforting for me to have him there.

Liz kindly took the long flight home with me. I was happy for her company, although I think I slept the whole way back to Texas.

In Austin I saw Dr. Doug Elenz, the surgeon who would repair my shattered collarbone. The first thing he did was compare the X-rays he took against the ones taken in Spain. Mark Higgins, my manager; Bill Stapleton, my agent; Anna; and I all seemed to share the same thought: <u>This is not good.</u>

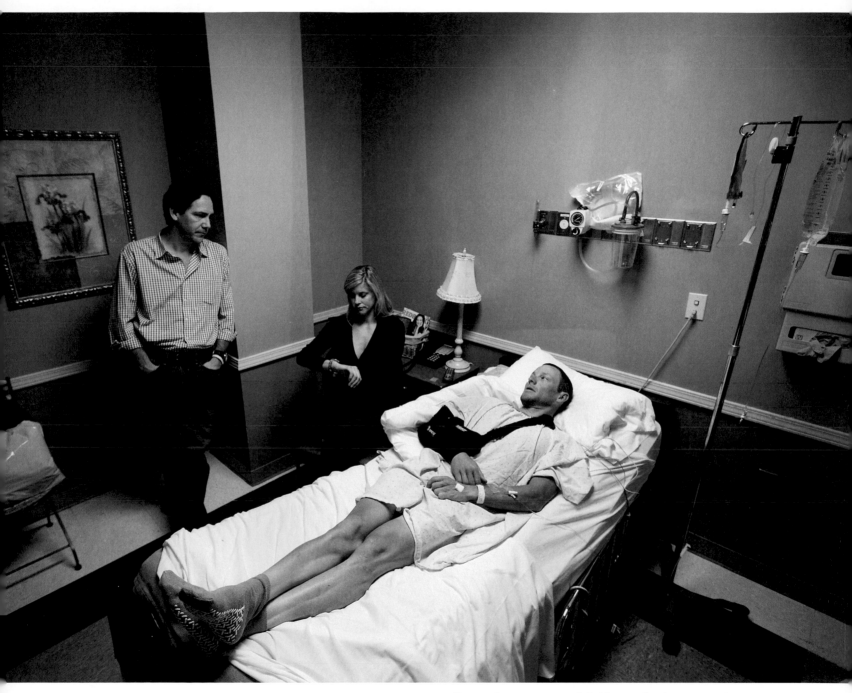

However, the surgery went well. Dr. Elenz got the plate in, put twelve screws in place, and instructed me to go home and not even think about riding for a week.

What Dr. Elenz didn't know was that I wasn't going to pay attention to his one-week rule. I got on the bike two days after the surgery. Anna caught me when she came home from running errands. Here she's smiling but that doesn't mean she was happy with me.

Dr. Elenz came to check on the SteriStrips used to seal up the incision.

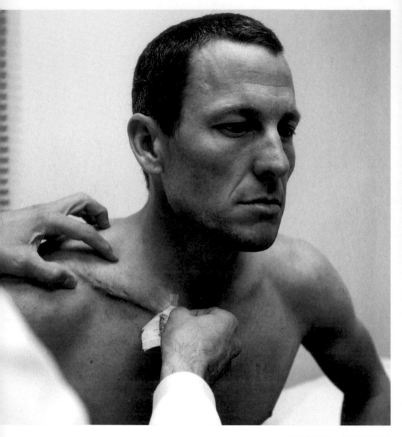

APRIL 2009
Here he is finally pulling the SteriStrips off.
That's one long scar.

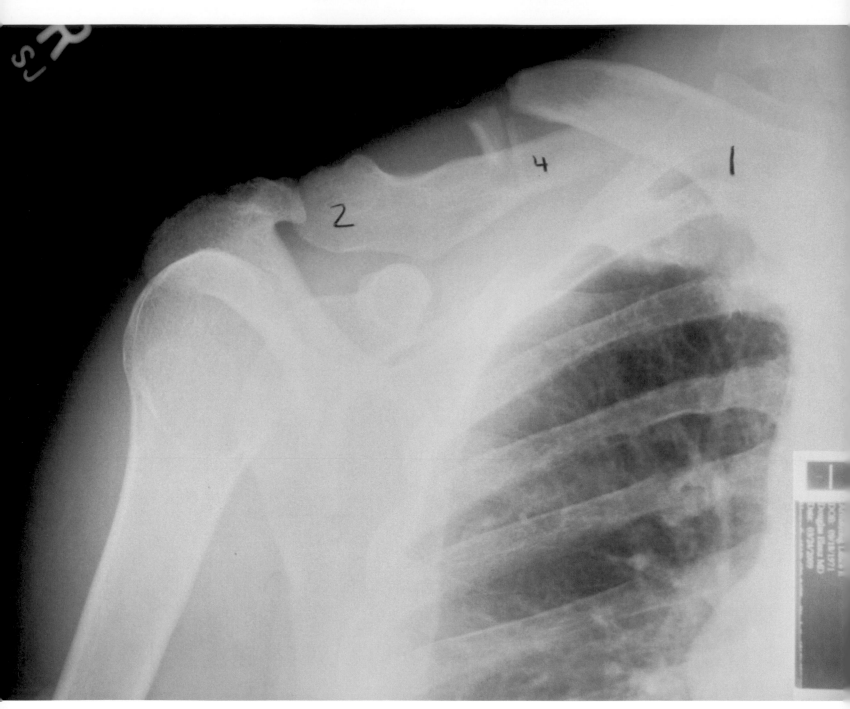

My "before" X-ray shows the breaks.

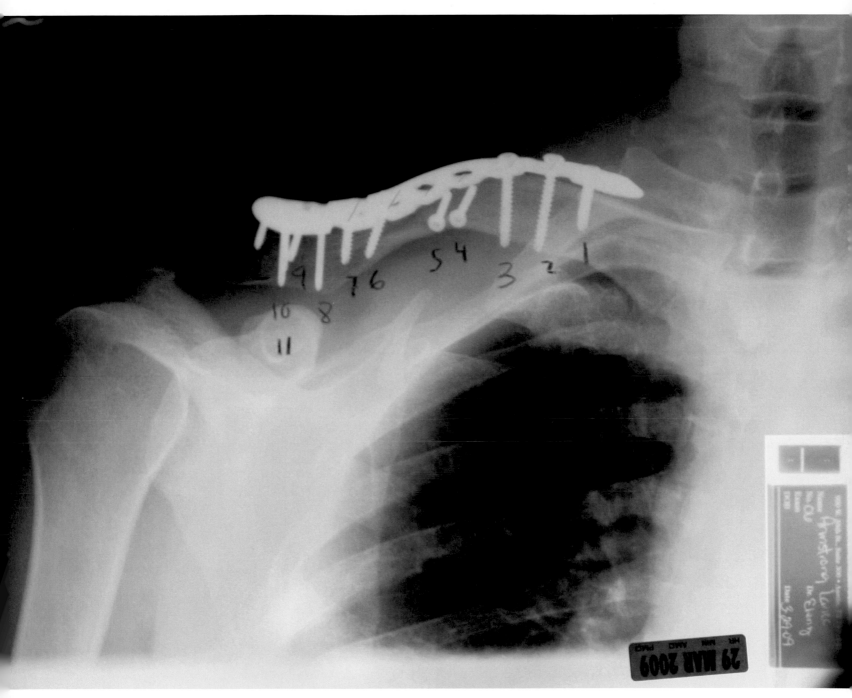

My "after" X-ray shows the plate and screws in place.

Back home in Aspen, I started training for the Giro d'Italia again. April can be tricky there, weather-wise. After a 75-degree day with nothing but sunshine, you might wake up the next morning to find snow on the ground. One day I walked out for my daily training ride and realized that I probably wouldn't be riding in Aspen later that day. Instead, I went on a training ride with Max Taam and Len Zanni in Glenwood Springs, where we knew it would be a bit warmer. Here I am looking up to the sky, thinking "WTF."

We loaded up the car to take my kids skiing at Aspen Highlands. They are beginners, so we set them up with lessons and they spent the day there.

In Glenwood Springs we found an old dirt road that was in good condition. The route was uphill; the closer I got to the top, the more snow there was. It was a little treacherous and it wouldn't have been fun to go down with that plate in my collarbone. I'm happy to report that my collarbone and I made it through that section of snow intact.

After the training ride, I drove back to Aspen and met the kids at the end of their ski lesson. I'm a bit of a geek dad: couldn't resist snapping photos of my kids skiing down the hill.

Getting ready for baby and practicing my rocking skills. We chose not to know beforehand if our child was going to be a boy or a girl. We had a few names picked out for both, and the nursery was gender neutral.

We headed to New Mexico for the Tour of the Gila, a great old American race that has been around for decades. This is an old-school American bike race, where teams show up and stay either at really small hotels or with hosts. Chris Horner, Levi, and I rode as Team Mellow Johnny's, named for my bike shop in Austin. Levi was as unbeatable here as he was in California. The three of us totaled up our age at the race, and realized we had more than a hundred years combined. We were proud to clean up over the young guys.

We had a great dinner at our host house. With me here are Johan Bruyneel, Higs, College, Levi, and Bart Knaggs (with his back to the camera).

An entrepreneurial kid showed up at the Tour of the Gila with giant printed cutouts of my face. He had hundreds, maybe even thousands, of these and was selling them for five dollars apiece. They were a popular item. It was freaky to see hundreds of cutouts of my face bobbing around town that weekend. I took the opportunity to grab one from somebody and do a group shot with my clones.

The Giro, Baby Max, and Tour Prep

MAY 2009

Before the start of the Giro, I went to Rome for some key meetings with members of the Italian government, including the minister of foreign affairs, Franco Frattini. We discussed cancer in Italy as well as the G8 summit, which Italy was hosting that year.

After the team presentation for the Giro, we were taken to a press conference via gondola. Riding in style! I'd never really been to Venice before. What a stunning city.

The Giro started with a 20-kilometer team time trial, which is pretty rare. We were the underdogs for this. No one had us pegged for greatness. But we had a good team on paper, and if we could be good technically we could perform well. We didn't win, but we were close. We got third. It was a nice day for me, because it was my first big race after breaking my collarbone and I felt strong. Johan insisted that I come across the finish first. I sprinted my ass off to get around Jani.

The Giro winds through snowcapped mountains. That's what I'd come to Italy for: to get used to riding with the peloton every day and getting along with the guys.

Later I looked through the race book with Chris Horner, whom I nicknamed "Redneck." Chris is a great teammate and was particularly helpful to me this year.

This stage went from Austria, then back into Italy via Switzerland and St. Moritz. We were riding on some of the roads I trained on extensively before most Tours de France. I often spent the entire month of June in St. Moritz before the Tour.

I was having trouble getting my position as comfortable as I like so I asked my mechanic Chris Van Roosbroeck to take some measurements and make some adjustments.

On the morning of the ninth stage, I had a meeting with Dario Cioni, representing the Professional Cyclists Association. We were discussing the safety of a particularly dangerous stage that had train tracks running in the direction of the course and cars parked in the middle of the road. The riders decided to stage a boycott by not racing, only riding, this stage. Dario was asking me what we should do. Ultimately, we got a ruling from the UCI that the stage would be neutralized.

It's a tight squeeze but sometimes the back of the bus is the only place to stretch before a stage.

On this climb at Moncenisio, I am actually in front of the pink jersey worn by Danilo Di Luca, who went on to get second in the Giro but unfortunately was later disqualified after failing a drug test.

This fan is at most bike races that we do. I'm not sure what he does for a living. He alternates between the Armstrong jersey with longhorns, a Levi Leipheimer jersey with elk horns, and, more recently, a Tyler Farrar jersey with eagle wings coming out of the helmet. He's a great fan, a real supporter. The Europeans got a kick out of seeing him every day.

After the fourteenth stage, I had a special Q&A session when Fabio Casartelli's son Marco interviewed me for his school paper. His father was my teammate in 1995. Fabio suffered a horrible crash in the Tour and died. Marco was a month old when Fabio passed away. I've stayed close to Marco and Fabio's widow, Annalisa. They're very dear friends.

A lighter moment with Chechu: having a big ol' plate of pasta with a glass of red wine.

The following day, we raced the shortest stage: only 83 kilometers.

     Signing in that day in the piazza at Avellino not so far from Naples. Even the sign-in board is cool at the Giro—it was transparent so the fans could see us check in.

The final time trial, in Rome. Seventy-five percent of the course was over cobble-stone streets. That's the Coliseum in the background. It was an absolutely stunning setting. Just before I was to ride, it started to rain. Wet cobblestones don't make for easy riding, but I have to say, I still really love Rome.

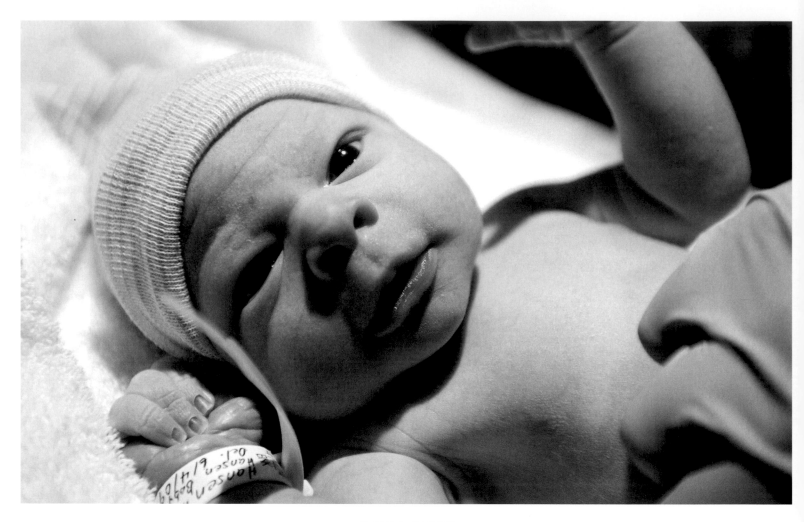

JUNE 2009

There was more than one comeback in 2009. For those who have followed my story, you know that after rounds and rounds of high-dose chemotherapy more than a decade ago I wasn't able to have children naturally, at least that's what we all thought. But miracles happen and something else came back in 2009. The result was the birth of Maxwell Edward Armstrong on June 4, 2009. This was a very special day, not just for Anna and me but for the whole family: Luke, Grace, Bella, my mom, and Kristin. This was a milestone for our family and also a beacon of hope for cancer survivors who dream of having families in the future. Max seemed happy to be here and unaware of his significance to the cancer survivor movement.

Luke is a wonderful big brother.

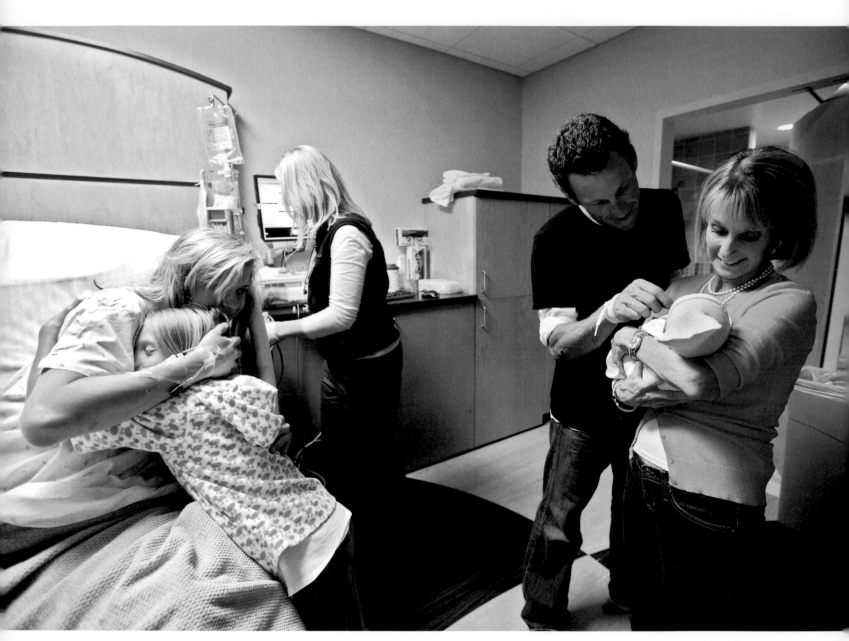

Hats off to the Aspen Hospital. It's a great place—very professional, very efficient, quiet. The staff made us feel at home. Anna got a big hug from Isabelle. My mom—without a doubt the best grandmother in the world—has Max.

And Bella was already babysitting.

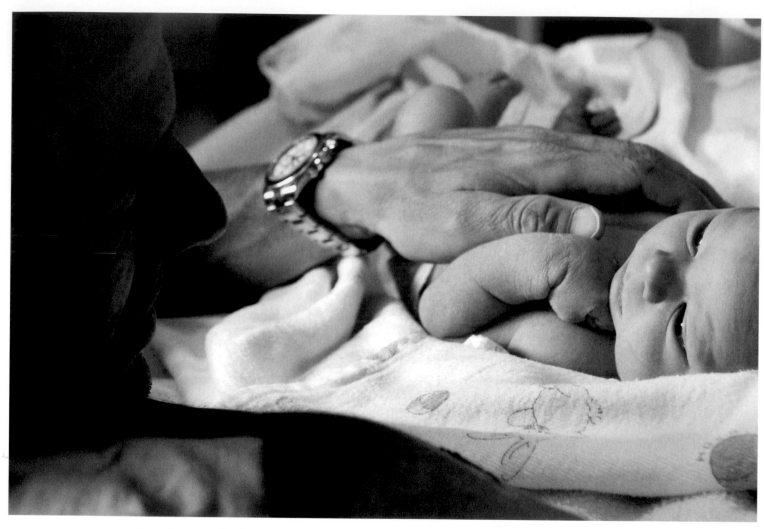

You realize how small and precious babies are when you can put your hand over their chest and pretty much cover them. Finally we were ready to take Max home. This was our last morning in the hospital. We were cleared for checkout and ready to go.

Back home, in the nursery,
the three of us relax while Anna nurses.

I spent the month of June recovering from the Giro, becoming a dad for the fourth time, and training for the Tour. Each morning I'd ride with Luke, Bella, and Grace to the day camp, where activities included urban bike riding, rock climbing, rafting, and fishing. After dropping them off, I'd do my training ride.

By the afternoon, I'd be settled in my office.

Another quiet moment with just Max and me. He is a very content baby, very relaxed, very quiet. He clearly has his mom's demeanor and she's happy about that. Nothing else seems to matter when he's in my arms.

Le Tour and Beyond:
From Monaco to Ireland

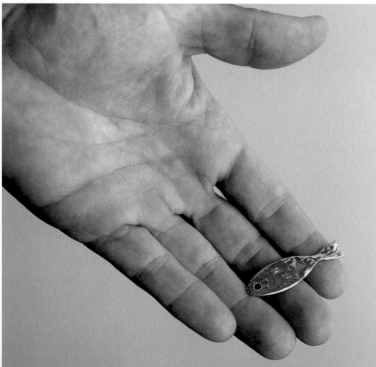

JULY 2009

In advance of the Tour de France, Nike sent me some limited-edition shoes, and Liz gave me a Tour onesy for Max—his very own <u>maillot jaune</u>.

My friend Michel Gamary, who ran a restaurant outside of Nice where I've trained, used to give me a little gift—a sort of good luck charm—at the start of the Tour. But by 2009 Michel had sold his restaurant and I had lost his number. I wasn't sure I was going to see him. Then at the presentation in Monte Carlo, all of a sudden there was Michel. He said he would meet me at 10:00 a.m. the next morning at my hotel with my traditional gift—this time a small gold fish that he'd had blessed by an Italian priest. I really appreciated his effort and kept this talisman with me for the entire Tour.

Prince Albert hosted an LAF event for us while we were in Monaco. He is an old friend of mine, a big fan of cycling, and a great supporter of the foundation. I'm very grateful for his hospitality.

It was a day or two before the start, riding my new time trial bike that artist Marc Newson designed for me. Clearly those legs were ready to race.

Always nice to have a visit from the greatest cyclist of all time. Eddy Merckx is not only a great friend; he's like a father to me. I really cherish our time together. We discussed the Tour. Eddy had some thoughts about how things might go. I'm so grateful for the way he's taken me under his wing.

This was a very big moment for me: the first time I had been on the start ramp of the Tour de France since 2005. You ride up the ramp and sign in right where I'm standing, and then you are held until the clock counts down and you start. I had so many emotions—I was nervous, happy, giddy, curious. More than anything I was very excited to be there. I think everyone watching could tell how much I wanted to be on that start line.

After my race, I went back to the hotel to watch the other favorites go off. I went early in the day, so I had to wait around for a few hours to find out how the others did. In the end, Fabian Cancellara proved to be just too strong. He wound up taking the yellow jersey.

There's quite a frenzy every day at the stage starts. I had a chat with Gérald Holtz of France 2. Nicolas Facq, in the sunglasses, is one of the two French-appointed security guards assigned to me for the Tour. He's a good man.

Later I had a more intimate interview. Philippe Maertens, our team public relations manager, is beside me.

My friend Ben Stiller stopped by before the team time trial. I'd set it up so he could ride in the team car with Johan. Ben had an idea for a funny home video. He hopped on my bike when it was on the wind trainer as if he was warming up. I'd come for my warm-up and he'd refuse to get off. When Ben finally did get off the bike, in a not-so-graceful way, he managed to torque the chain so much that it snapped. Mechanics had about four minutes to change it before the start. Could have been a total catastrophe. The good news is we wound up with a pretty funny video and my new chain held up fine for the stage.

In a lighter moment in my room before the team time trial, I discovered my inner Iron Maiden.

The team just crushed the team time trial, absolutely destroyed the field. Before the stage I was 30 or 40 seconds down. None of us thought we would win by enough to put me in the yellow jersey. But we ended up just 22/100ths of a second short. So I just missed the yellow jersey, and in this shot you can see that Cancellara has preserved it.

In interviews after the team time trial, I wasn't about to complain about not being in the yellow jersey, not when the team had nailed such an impressive victory.

Rick Reilly interviewed me later for ESPN. I've known Rick for a long time and am happy to call him a good friend. I am there on the massage table; Reilly has a nice view of my ass while Ryszard "Richard" Kielpinski gives me a great massage like he does every day. Higs is in the background on his BlackBerry, working like always.

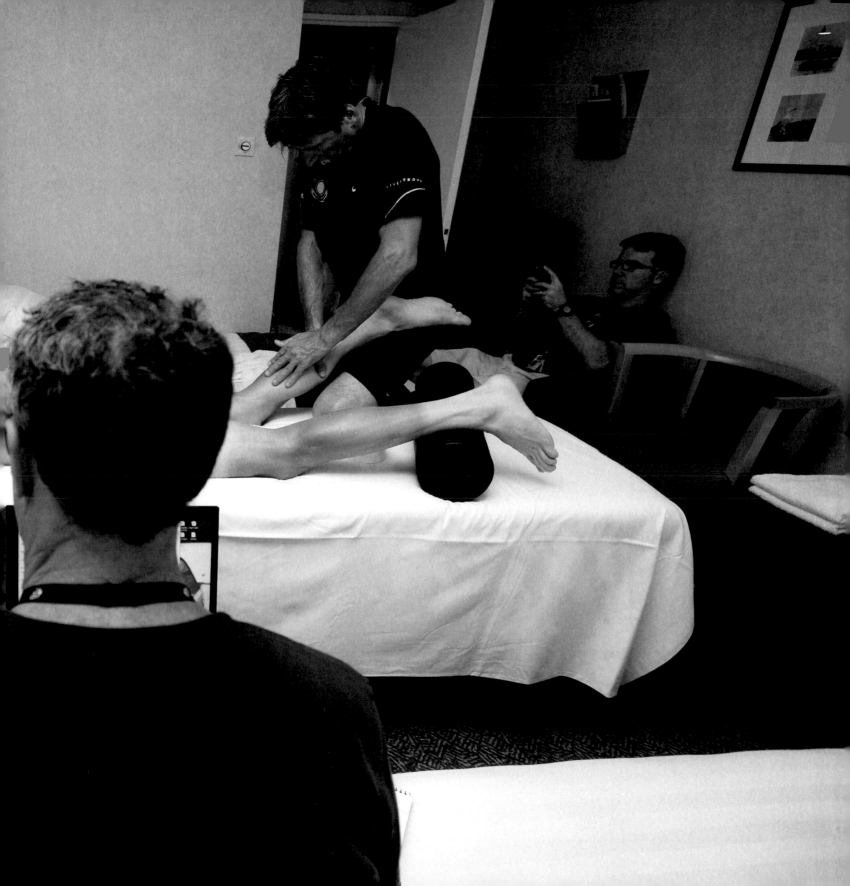

The stage into Purpan was very windy. The peloton ended up blowing apart due to crosswinds from the sea, but for this moment the field was still together.

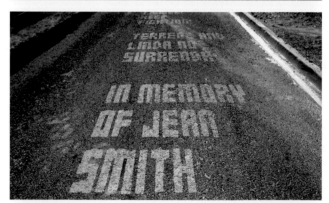

In the spirit of LIVE**STRONG**, Nike came up with a clever idea. They created a device that could print messages on the Tour course. Via this device, dubbed the Chalkbot, people could send shout-outs to loved ones dealing with cancer or in remembrance of those who had passed away from it. As we rode, we got to see these good wishes and be reminded of the LIVE**STRONG** message.

I always have a lot of visitors at the Tour. Frank Marshall, a great old friend of
mine and a fantastic movie producer, dropped by along with Jimmy Buffett. Bart,
my business manager; Bill; and I are all cracking up.

Cancellara had given over the jersey to an Italian rider, Rinaldo Nocentini. This was the first major uphill test of the Tour. I'm coming to the line here with Cadel Evans, Andy Schleck, Denis Menchov, Carlos Sastre, Bradley Wiggins, and Levi. Alberto had attacked a mile or two before this and was about fifteen seconds ahead of us.

This wasn't really the team plan, so I wasn't too happy at the finish.

Nocentini led us over the Col du Tourmalet, one of the most famous climbs of the Tour. It was super hot and, unfortunately, still a long way from the finish, so they neutralized the climb.

I love the pageantry of the Tour and the way the communities surrounding the route really get in the spirit. Here people have brought out their donkeys and dressed them in Tour jerseys.

The team meeting in the bus is a daily ritual. We look at the routes and study the course profiles. We talk about wind, road surface, the width of the road, and any little thing that might make a difference for that day's stage.

At the end of that stage, I had another surprise guest, Robin Williams. He has always been a great fan of the Tour and was on vacation in the area. He came by for a little chat and some laughs. A lot of people were curious about how Robin has done since his heart surgery a few months ago. I can tell you: he's funnier than ever. He really had me and Higs in hysterics at the Tour. He made fun of the plan to ban team radios. He was asking, "What's next? Smoke signals? Morse code? A pigeon flying up to land on your shoulder with a message?"

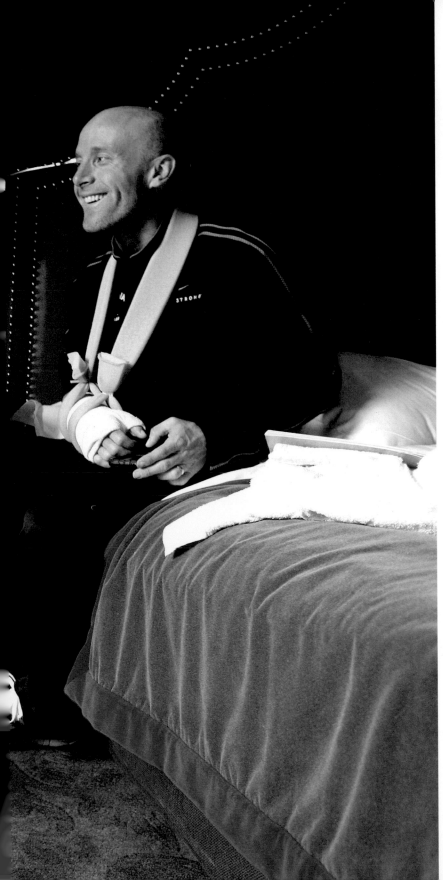

Levi had what seemed like a minor crash toward the end of the previous day's stage, but he landed hard on his wrist. At dinner that night he had trouble picking up his fork. He went to bed thinking he would wake up feeling better. Instead, he woke up in a lot of pain. X-rays showed that his wrist was fractured. He stopped by my room to let me know what was going on and have a quick chat. Despite his pain and the disappointment over having to leave the Tour, you can see we were still having a good time. I think right here I was encouraging him to get his wrist healed so I could thoroughly kick his ass at the Leadville 100 just a month later.

Nearly every day on the Tour you'd find Alain Gallopin and Johan Bruyneel in the team car, with Alain studying the map and Johan talking to the riders.

I dropped back at one point to talk to Johan about the race. Next to me is my teammate Gregory Rast, from Switzerland, who was with me most days during the Tour protecting me from the wind and the elements.

Here's the breakfast of champions: Nutella, an Italian product that is the European equivalent of peanut butter. Kids in Europe grow up eating Nutella, a delicious concoction of cocoa and hazelnut. I have it every morning for breakfast.

Even on rest days we go on easy training rides. There was a fair amount of tension in our the team at this point, so it seemed ironic to see a sign for "Happyland."

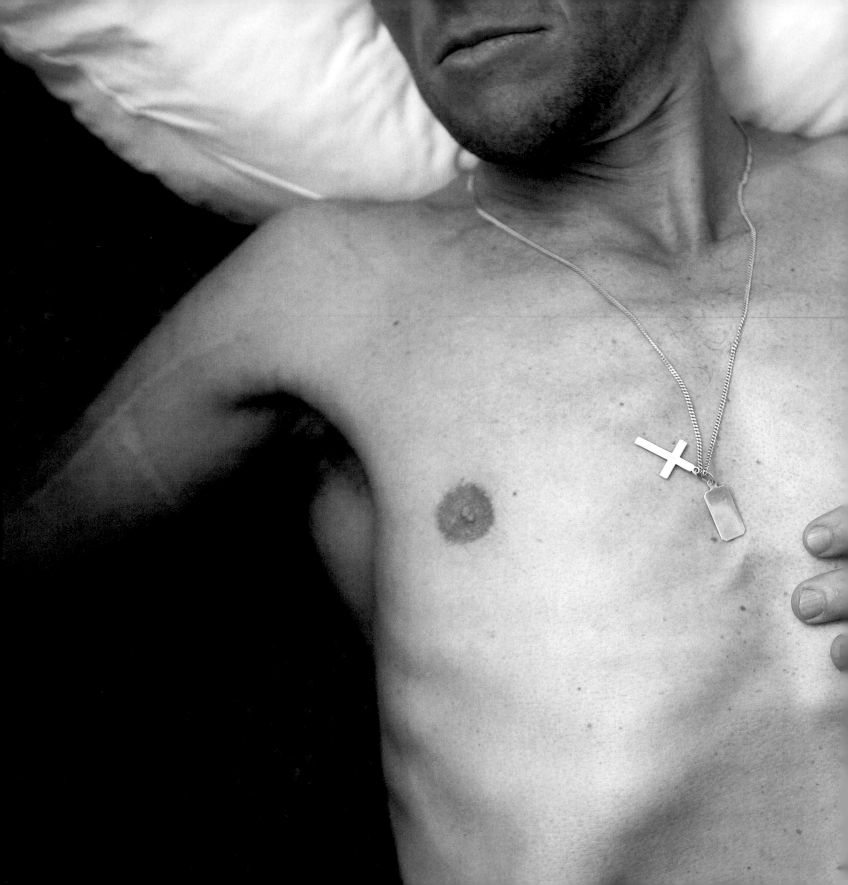

This is a shot of the necklace I have worn for all of my Tours. Stacy Pounds, who was Bill's assistant back when I was diagnosed, gave the cross to me. She was incredibly supportive during that time, which meant a lot to me and my family. She helped manage my cancer treatment. Unfortunately, just as I was finishing my treatment, Stacy was diagnosed with lung cancer. We exchanged crosses and wore them as a symbol of our solidarity with and affection for each other; to this day I wear the cross she gave me. Stacy wasn't as fortunate as I was in her battle with cancer. After she passed away she was buried with the cross I'd given her.

The other medallion I wear is one my ex-wife Kristin gave me. I rely on and trust her immensely. She is a very spiritual woman. This medallion is inscribed with a verse from the Bible, Second Timothy, chapter 4, verse 7:

I have fought the good fight.
I have finished the race.
I have kept the faith.

Coming down Great St. Bernard is a sweeping switch-back. The team is riding tempo on the front, with me, Alberto, and Wiggins following.

I was more pleased with my ride on the longer Alpine climbs than I was at Verbier. Even when I fell back on that day's last climb, the Little St. Bernard, I caught my breath and easily jumped back to Alberto's group. I was feeling better.

On the days we had rain at the Tour—the stages into Barcelona and Colmar—it was always slippery, and it was wet on the early part of that next stage. We knew it was going to be a hard day, so we rode an easy tempo up the first climb, the Roselend. That first downhill was real sketchy in the rain.

2009 was significant in that for the first time, perhaps, French fans and I enjoyed a great relationship. It was fun to see supportive signs, like this one some kids had made that translates roughly to "Armstrong climbs on the moon."

I made only one mistake in the Alps, and that was on the second to last climb of this seventeenth stage. I decided not to go with the Schleck brothers when they attacked on the Col de Romme—which was the steepest, nastiest climb of the Tour.

Andreas Klöden and Alberto went with them, but I was afraid of the accelerations. I stayed back with the other contenders, but I should have just gone. I was strong on the final climb, the Colombière, and dropped the others during the last kilometer. I finished that stage in Le Grand-Bornand—where I won a Tour stage in 2004—with the young Italian Vincenzo Nibali. But the two minutes I lost there would cost me second place on the podium.

Throughout 2009 I invited some of my favorite contemporary artists to participate in Nike's "Stages" art tour. Shepard Fairey, Marc Newson, Yoshitomo Nara, KAWS, Kenny Scharf, and Damien Hirst all came through. Some of them painted bikes I rode on. Ultimately, these bikes and artwork will be auctioned off to benefit the LAF. This particular morning I got my first real look at the bike Damien Hirst produced for my ride into Paris. Hirst is a phenomenal artist and I was blown away by the level of detail and passion that went into this frame.

We stayed in some great hotels during the Tour, and Le Palace de Menthon on Lake Annecy was one of them. You can see the effects of the Tour on me: not much fat left.

The trials are always important, but this one was particularly significant for me because my family was arriving from the United States. After their plane landed they drove right to the time trial, where I was in the middle of warming up, and Luke immediately gave me a big hug.

I was so glad to hold little Max again.
In the three weeks since I'd last seen him,
he'd become a new man.

Grace and Bella watched me warm up. As if I needed any more motivation for a time trial; all I had to do was look over and see my two girls. Made me feel really good.

Andreas Klöden is the rider in the middle that I'm reaching out my hand to. He spent many years riding in support of Jan Ullrich, who was often my biggest rival. So we were longtime adversaries—until this year when we found ourselves on the same team. We quickly struck up a friendly bond. Andreas is a talented rider and total team player. My buddy Dave Ellsweig from Aspen is holding Max.

Heading down the start ramp in Annecy. An important day. I'm trying to hold onto a podium spot. Didn't have a great time trial, but did well enough to keep me in contention.

Anna, Max, and I enjoy a calm moment back in the hotel overlooking Lake Annecy.

This is probably a shot that not many people saw on TV. For those who thought I never rode in support of Alberto, I think this says it all. There was no one else left on the team by this point, so I had to do my job and protect the yellow jersey for him.

A quiet moment with Carlos Sastre before the final stage.

Top of Ventoux, the Giant of Provence, as they say, arguably the hardest climb in France, harder than Alpe d'Huez and Col du Tourmalet. This was a defining moment for me in this Tour. This was the day that I either held on to my podium spot or didn't. I think the general consensus, even among the experts, was that I wouldn't hold onto it. Fortunately, I was able to stay with the young guns and preserve third place going into Paris.

Glad to be heading down Ventoux as the media strained to get a shot.

Andreas and I shared a seat on the train from Ventoux to Paris for the final stage. Notice the cover of L'Équipe. Most people know that L'Équipe hasn't exactly been kind to me in the past. But check out the headline, "Chapeau, Le Texan," which translates as "Hats Off to the Texan." I think we are all good now, and looking forward to 2010.

The final stage into Paris, with the Arc de Triomphe in the back, on the Champs-Élysées, one of the most famous boulevards in the world. I was so proud to be riding that beautiful Damien Hirst bike.

The final podium with Andy Schleck, Alberto, and me. I guess I am looking up at the trophy. I have seven of them; I know what it's like to have one, to hold it up, to hear your national anthem. It's a very significant thing in cycling, and in sport. Alberto was better than any of us in this Tour, and he deserved to win. Having said that, I look forward to coming back and going for number eight.

Stepping off the final podium, I spotted Grace clapping for me. Other supporters included Luke; my mom; Anna; Max; and mom's husband, Ed. It was great to be with them all again after several weeks apart.

I think the kids were wondering who the guy wearing Dad's jersey was.

With my girls and Luke. I was looking forward to spending a lot of time with these three—and with Max and Anna.

Had to thank the policemen on the motorcycles who had been with us the whole Tour. They'd been away from their families for three weeks—all to keep us safe on the roads.

Ed Ruscha is one of the artists who contributed to the Nike "Stages" tour. I'm a big fan. I love the piece you see here—so much so that I bought it. It was great to have Ed in Paris at the Nike "Stages" event that evening.

I enjoyed a little toast with my new pal Andreas and our team.

Some would argue that this is where the comeback all started, and I would agree. The Leadville 100 in 2008 was the moment that I stood on the start line at a race, threw my leg over the top tube, looked down the road, and got that feeling of what it was like to be in a race again. I immediately had that feeling of excitement, those butterflies—nerves—and I said to myself, "My god, I love this." In 2009, it was important to me to come back and honor that experience by racing it again. I had a great day, rode 65 miles alone, and, as you can see on the right, made it through the last ten miles with a flat tire. It was a real honor to race with Dave Wiens, an American mountain bike hero. He's won this race six times.

The LIVE**STRONG** Global Cancer Summit in Dublin, Ireland, represented the culmination of our yearlong efforts. This was another reason that I decided to come back: to talk about cancer from a global perspective in communities, tribes, countries, continents, and cultures that don't normally discuss the disease. With sixty-nine countries present, five hundred people in attendance, and four billion dollars committed, this was our Super Bowl. I think everyone there was moved by the participants' dedication and passion—especially me.

While I was in Ireland I decided to go on a bike ride in beautiful Phoenix Park. I thought it would be fun to invite other cyclist to join me, so I did, via Twitter. I didn't expect that about 1,200 people would show up for the ride! This is a candid shot of me with the group that responded to my Tweet. I loved seeing who showed up, from the guy with a yellow jersey on and a city bike with a horn, to the girl who had her bike lock wrapped around her head tube. This was my favorite bike ride of the year.

Anna—for that steady, loving force in my life.

To **Kik**—thanks for your prayers, your blessing, your friendship, and for being an incredible mom.

Johan—for the best sports coach/manager that the world has ever seen.

Liz—for coming along on this journey and always keeping it easy.

Doug—for being the best and brightest mind in "our" fight. The fight against cancer.

The team at LAF—pound for pound the best organization in the world.

To my fellow survivors—for providing the level of support that only millions can do. I constantly feel your presence.

Bill, Bart, Higs, Caroline, Karly, Laura, and Mary Grace—for keeping this thing running efficiently and letting me focus on one thing.

And, finally, **my teammates**—without you guys—riders and staff—none of this would be possible. I can't wait for 2010!

—Lance Armstrong

Thanks to:

My husband, **James Bonney,** for your love and unwavering support.

My parents, **Linda and Chuck Kreutz,** for encouraging me to go after my dreams.

My brothers, **Matthew and Nathan,** for being my Tour de France assistants/Sherpas/chauffeurs and for always looking out for me.

Baby Bonney for a wonderful pregnancy that spanned eight countries!

Johan Bruyneel and the Astana team and staff for making me feel like part of the family.

Moto drivers, **Corey Yeaton, Brian Stephens, Brian O'Grady, Jim Faria, Serg Seynave, Diego Hartmann, Steve Farris, David McIver, Blair Jones,** and **Chad Cunningham.** Thank you, **Kelly Cunningham,** for lending me your protective moto gear just when I needed it most!

Dave Bolch for your awesome driving skills in the car and on the moto and for introducing me to the Deutsch Apple Bakery.

Margie Wargo for your friendship and for bringing a smile to my "Poker Face" on the road.

Deborah Cannon and Taylor Jones for your invaluable photographic insight and friendship.

University of Texas photography professors **Rick Williams,** for encouraging me to switch my major to photojournalism, and **J. B. Colson** for believing I had something special to offer the photography world.

Mike Owen at Canon Europe for the two incredible Mark III 1Ds camera bodies.

Rip Esselstyn for introducing me to Richard and your enthusiasm.

Richard Pine at InkWell Management.

The Touchstone Team, especially Stacy Creamer, Lauren Spiegel, Ruth Lee-Mui, Joy O'Meara, Twisne Fan, Allison Brennan, Fausto Bozza, Martha Schwartz, Cherlynne Li, and Jason Heuer.

Capital Sports and Entertainment, especially Bill Stapleton and Caroline Vander Ark for your hard work and essential contributions on this project.

Lance for inviting me to document your historic comeback year. I'm so grateful for your loyal support, professional respect, and dear friendship. Thank you for the project of a lifetime. I have enjoyed the ride!

—Elizabeth Kreutz

Lance Armstrong

is a seven-time winner of the Tour de France and full-time cancer fighter. He is the chairman and founder of the LIVE**STRONG** Foundation, a nonprofit organization that assists cancer patients around the world with managing and surviving the disease. In 2008, Armstrong was named one of Time magazine's 100 Most Influential People. He is the author of It's Not About the Bike and Every Second Counts. He lives in Austin, Texas. To find out more about Lance Armstrong and the Lance Armstrong Foundation, visit www.livestrong.org and www.livestrong.com.

©Madison Morales

Elizabeth Kreutz

is an independent photojournalist specializing in documentary sports photography. She has traveled around the world and has been granted exclusive access to photograph Lance Armstrong and the Discovery and Astana cycling teams. She also has photographed the 2006 Winter Olympics in Turin and the 2008 Summer Olympics in Beijing. Her work has been featured in world-leading publications including Newsweek, Sports Illustrated, and USA Today. She lives in Austin, Texas, with her husband, James Bonney, and they are expecting their first child in December. To find out more about Elizabeth Kreutz's work, visit www.elizabethkreutz.com.

For this special collector's edition of Comeback 2.0,
I've included this extra selection of some of my favorite photos from my comeback year.
LIVE**STRONG**.

—Lance

RETIREMENT
IS FOR THOSE
WHO CANNOT
WIN THE TOUR

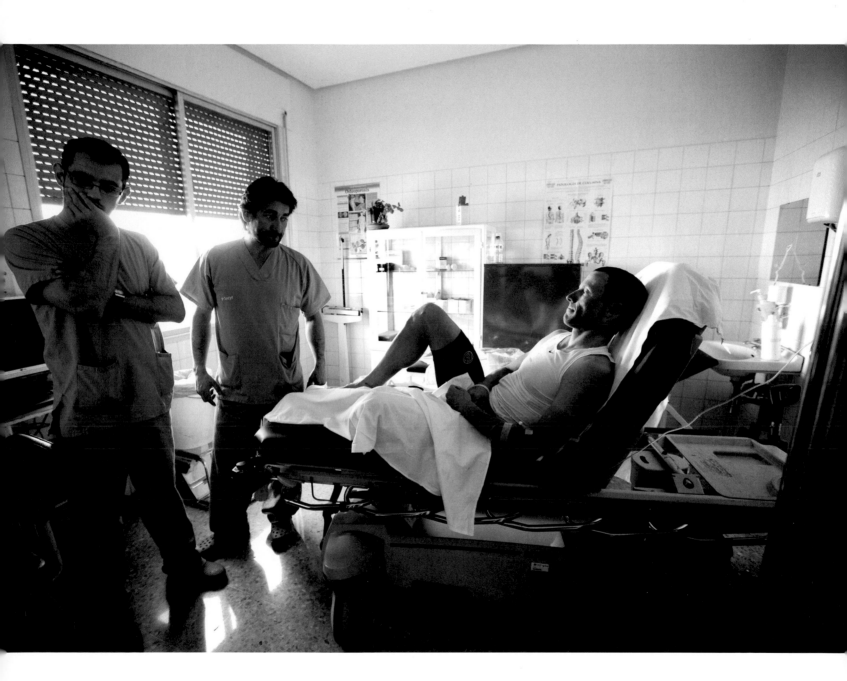